ACKNOWLEDGMENT OF COUNTRY

I acknowledge the First Nations people, the Jagera and Turrbal people, and their land on which I write. I acknowledge past, present, and emerging leaders who have walked and continue to walk and honour this land. I acknowledge the First Nations people of Australia as the oldest continuous culture. I acknowledge the First Nations people of Australia as custodians of the oldest continuous spirituality.

SOUL MURMURINGS

LIVING WITH GRACE, HUMILITY, AND INTEGRITY

ANDREW KENNELLY

Published by Wilkinson Publishing Pty Ltd
ACN 006 042 173
PO Box 24135, Melbourne, VIC 3001, Australia
Ph: +61 3 9654 5446
enquiries@wilkinsonpublishing.com.au
www.wilkinsonpublishing.com.au

Follow Wilkinson Publishing on social media.

WilkinsonPublishing
wilkinsonpublishinghouse
WPBooks

© Copyright Andrew Kennelly 2024

All rights reserved. No part of this publication may be reproduced, stored in a retrieval system or transmitted in any form by any means without the prior permission of the copyright owner. Enquiries should be made to the publisher.

Every effort has been made to ensure that this book is free from error or omissions. However, the Publisher, the Authors, the Editor or their respective employees or agents, shall not accept responsibility for injury, loss or damage occasioned to any person acting or refraining from action as a result of material in this book whether or not such injury, loss or damage is in any way due to any negligent act or omission, breach of duty or default on the part of the Publisher, the Authors, the Editor, or their respective employees or agents.

ISBN: 9781922810588
A catalogue record for this book is available from the National Library of Australia.

Edited by Ian Mathieson, iEdit

iEdit

Cover and internal design by Jo Hunt

Printed in China

We are all visitors to this time, this place. We are just passing through.
Our purpose here is to observe, to learn, to grow, to love …
and then we return home.

AUSTRALIAN ABORIGINAL SAYING

CONTENTS

Acknowledgment of Country	ii
Introduction – a Lunar Moment	1
What is Spirituality?	1
The Who, Why, and How of the Book	2
Terminology	3
PART ONE	5
Listening to our Soul Murmurings	5
Spirituality of Stillness	6
1. An Historical Quest	6
2. Meandering River	8
3. Caring for a Newborn	10
4. Residing in the Shadows	12
5. A Wonderful Gift	14
6. A Simple Way	16
7. Electric Train	18
8. Our Three Closest Friends	20
9. On the Terrace	22
10. Lamb and a Clare Valley Red	24
Spirituality in the Arts and Travel	26
11. A Place of Restful Contemplation	26
12. A Doorway to the Soul	28
13. It's Not Your Fault	30
14. Discovering My Home	32
15. Look at the View, Kiddies	34

Spirituality in Death, Grief and Challenges of Life	36
16. Walking With Death	36
17. If I Had One Day	38
18. Good Grief	40
19. Upside Down and Inside Out	42
Spirituality and Religion	44
20. The Distinction	44
21. Talking Symbols	46
22. The Silly Present	48
23. The Four Elements	50
24. The Good, the Bad, and the Ugly	52
25. The Pews Are Empty	54
PART TWO	57
Acting on our Soul Murmurings	57
Spirituality of Harmony	58
26. The Contradiction	58
Spirituality and the Illuminators: Grace, Humility and Integrity	60
27. Grace – A Noble Quest	60
28. The Challenge	62
29. Humility – Grounded in the Earth	64
30. Integrity – To Be Whole	66
31. Creating a Wave	68
The Spirituality of Sexuality	70
32. A Tale of an Old Friar	70
33. We Are Beautiful	72

34. Illuminating Love	74
35. An Intimate Partnership	76
Spirituality at Work	**78**
36. The Lunchbox	78
37. My Opus	80
38. A Calling to Serve	82
39. The Highest Priority	84
Discovering Spirituality in Our Parenting	**86**
40. The Green Cathedral	86
41. Reimagining	88
42. Letting Go	90
43. The Expert	92
44. Building Blocks	94
The Spirituality of Social Action	**96**
45. Making a Difference	96
46. In Exile	98
47. Engagement	100
Big Picture Spirituality	**102**
48. The Light and Shade	102
49. Holding Opposites	104
50. Surfing Lessons	106
51. Legacy	108
52. Touchstones	110
Conclusion	112
Acknowledgments	115
Andrew Kennelly – My Story	117

INTRODUCTION
– A LUNAR MOMENT

It was a cold July winter's night in my home town of Melbourne. The year was 1969, the year of the moon landing. My oldest sister, Barbara, took me out into the back yard to see the full moon. Jokingly she asked me if I could see any of the astronauts. I was turning nine in September, old enough to understand her humour.

After we had marvelled at the achievements of the three American astronauts, my sister went inside and I stayed a little while, staring at the Milky Way. It was a profound moment. For the first time in my short life, I had allowed myself to take in the immensity of the universe. I had this sense of awe and wonder. It was magical and mystifying. I was taken beyond myself. I was not sure what I was experiencing but I knew it was special.

Looking back now, I would define it as a spiritual moment.

WHAT IS SPIRITUALITY?

I invite you to pause and bring into your awareness a time when you felt totally alive, connected, and in awe of the beauty and mystery of life. It could be an experience had on your own, in your lover's arms, with friends, in a rainforest, in a chapel or mosque, or in the stillness of meditation.

What was the experience like and what words do you put around this event? Are there words? Did the experience take you beyond yourself?

We all have these special moments of insight and revelation.

These experiences inform us there is something beneath our immediate understanding of the world. While my 1969 lunar experience was initially received through my senses and rational mind, it penetrated another part of my being.

What label do we place on this intangible, 'other part of being'? I call it the soul. The place where we process these deeper experiences and hear the murmurs of our inner life. Spirituality is about these whispers. By attending to and listening to our soul, we come to a better understanding of who we are, and our mission in life.

My definition of spirituality is: the experience of listening and acting on the murmurings rumbling deep within us.

THE WHO, WHY, AND HOW OF THE BOOK

This book is for all people curious about the internal world. I hope it appeals in equal yet different measures to those of us from a faith-based background and those who have never and will never be connected to any form of religion.

The purpose of the book is to provide a creative, relevant, and practical way for us to explore the gentle movements and insights of our soul.

The book is divided into two sections. Part One explores how to listen to our murmurings, through stillness, the arts, travel, philosophy, ritual, symbol, and religion. Part Two explores how listening to our murmurings propels us to live a life that is quite different in motivation as I examine the illuminators, sexuality, the workplace, leaders, parenting, and social action. The final chapters explore the big picture of nationhood, the ocean, legacy and touchstones.

Each chapter is one page in length and finishes with suggestions for personal reflection and activity. These suggestions range from journalling, being still, viewing a movie, reading a book, engaging with the physical and external world and pondering specific questions. Each chapter has a blank page for thoughts, journalling, doodling, and reflections.

There are 52 chapters, one for each week of the year to provide quality time for practising and completing the activities suggested. My reflections are deliberately brief in length so there is ample time to digest them. The most benefit will be found in our personal reflection time.

As each chapter has its own theme and activity, chapters also can be read randomly without following any sequence.

My deepest wish is in reading this book we will feel more equipped and confident in listening to our murmurings; inspired to live a life of grace, humility, and integrity.

TERMINOLOGY

In the book, I use certain key terms with the following specific meanings.

Soul refers to our inner self, inner life, or spiritual self; the internal place that lies underneath our immediate understanding of the world. Soul in this context does not refer to a religious reality and is not connected to sin or salvation.

Soul murmurings refers to the gentle movements and insights we perceive during significant moments and in times of stillness and quiet. This term is interchangeable with soul whispers.

Quiet time refers to periods in our day where we deliberately choose to stop and listen to our soul murmurings. This term is interchangeable with soul time, soul work, soul moment, and being still.

Illuminators refers to the values of grace, humility, and integrity. These qualities gently emerge as we listen to our soul murmurings.

Grace refers to being courteous, gentle and grateful to ourselves and others. The term is interchangeable with being gracious.

Humility refers to being honest, respectful, and modest with ourselves and others. It recognises that we are neither sinner or saint and neither greater nor less than any other individual.

Integrity refers to being whole or complete. To be true to ourselves and others. It calls us to embrace our vulnerabilities. This term is interchangeable with authenticity.

Parent refers to all people who fulfill a parenting role, whether there is a biological relationship or not.

PART ONE

LISTENING TO OUR SOUL MURMURINGS

SPIRITUALITY OF STILLNESS

1. An Historical Quest

*The greatest use of a life is to spend
it on something that will outlast it.*

WILLAM JAMES

In Western and Eastern spirituality there has always been a hunger to understand and appreciate the depth of the human spirit. This quest has a long history of using meditation; the ability to be still.

We cannot be sure when the intentional act of being still first commenced in human history. Maybe it began with the hunters and gatherers as they gazed to the heavens or into their campfires. This we will never know. We note from historical records development of meditation in the Hindu, Buddhist, and Taoist traditions was at least 1500 years before the birth of Christianity.

We see the first signs of documented meditation in the West by Philo of Alexandria, and are aware of meditation practices in both the Jewish and Christian traditions, these becoming well-established in the Middle Ages.

Given this very brief expose of the origins of meditation, we can appreciate when we go to our sessions of yoga, mindfulness, meditative breathing, religious rituals, and tai chi, we are connecting to people and movements dating back to the dawn of human history. We are continuing an innate human enterprise seeking to travel inwards.

> REFLECT – You are not alone as you embark on this journey, many have gone before. Remember this history. How and when do you find quiet time, soul time, in your life? What is your relationship with silence?
>
> ACTION – Find a quiet place where you can be alone and sit for five minutes. Do nothing and be still. How did you experience those five minutes? Record your thoughts, experience and insights. Read *The Dreaming Path*, Paul Callaghan with Uncle Paul Gordon.

JOURNAL REFLECTIONS

2. Meandering River

If you try to change it, you will ruin it,
Try to hold it, and you will lose it.
TAO TE CHING

Being still and listening to our soul murmurings requires very gentle hands, allowing for movement and creativity. The way of the inner life is like the flow of a river meandering through a flood plain, bending and winding until a path is discovered. It cannot be dammed or corralled because it is the soul that directs us.

Like the meandering river, our journey inward requires us to flow with the natural movement of our energy. Resilience is required as we are challenged to let go of our preconceived ideas of the world and ourselves, and listen to the quiet movement of the river within.

The internal river understands the path on which we need to embark. It simply knows. Trust this process. Eventually, the river flows into the ocean and to an abundance of life. If we stay true to the journey, we will share in this abundance.

REFLECT – Do you connect to the image of the meandering river? Are you drawn to water? Is water a meaningful or poignant symbol for you? Does it speak to your soul? If not, what other images are significant for you?

ACTION – In your quiet time, connect with water in a way relevant for you. Listen to *River Song*, by Archie Roach. Watch and reflect on the movie *Empire Strikes Back*, and its explanation of 'The Force'.

JOURNAL REFLECTIONS

3. Caring for a Newborn

To love oneself is the beginning
of a lifelong romance.
OSCAR WILDE

When approaching our soul, we do this as if we were approaching a newborn child. The movement is with love and gratitude. On first meeting, our spiritual self recoils from loud obtrusive noises and gestures, just as a newborn child does. Instead, it responds to a warm embrace and a soothing voice.

As the soul becomes accustomed to our presence, it gradually feels greater confidence in revealing its secrets. Once the rapport between us and the inner life is established, the bond may quickly deepen.

As any parent knows, the best way to attend to a newborn child is to observe, listen, and act. Parents will often remark there are different cries for diverse needs. A cry for "I am hungry", a cry for "I need a change", and a cry for, "I just want a cuddle". In time the attuned parent can decipher these different signals and respond appropriately.

Meeting and attending to our spiritual self is no different. It is the ability to spend time with ourselves, to listen to the yearnings voiced in the silence. As with parenting, this is not an overnight process, it is a journey.

> REFLECT – Attuning yourself to the movement of your internal rhythm is about being a loving presence, just as a mother is to her newborn.
>
> ACTION – Continue your soul work by sitting quietly and becoming aware of your breath and heartbeat. Notice what happens. Hold yourself gently. After sitting quietly for a period of time, begin to write, draw, or doodle about this experience of stillness.

JOURNAL REFLECTIONS

4. Residing in the Shadows

> A single sunbeam is enough to
> drive away many shadows.
> FRANCIS OF ASSISI

Our soul does not respond to the cold clinical light of media coverage, psychological intervention, or left-brain logical thought. It shrinks into itself to avoid being exposed and negatively judged. The spiritual self cannot be forced to reveal itself.

John O'Donoghue in his book *Anam Cara*, contends the inner life responds more to the gentle candlelight that illuminates a darkened room. In this muted light, the soul reveals its rich store of wisdom and allows for mysteries and questions to dance unheeded.

Watch how people are drawn to the dance of a campfire. They are drawn not only to its warmth, colour, and movement but to its primeval call to a deeper awareness. The call of the soul is a part of who we are, and it is in the filtered light that murmurs emerge.

> REFLECT – For centuries the gentle power of candlelight or firelight, has been recognised as sacred by mystics and religious leaders. There can be no light without darkness. Your internal life understands the dichotomy of this union.
>
> ACTION – When the house is still at night, light a candle in the darkness, and watch the flame. Allow yourself to be still. In this partially illuminated space, the echo of your soul can be heard. Journal this experience. Read John Donohue's *Anam Cara: Spiritual Wisdom from the Celtic World*, where he writes about the soul residing in the shadows.

JOURNAL REFLECTIONS

5. A Wonderful Gift

Time itself comes in drops.
WILLIAM JAMES

The Vietnamese Zen Buddhist, Thich Nhat Hanh, suggests the first task in learning to be still is to simply become aware of our breath.

Watch and attend to ourselves as we breathe in, and breathe out. There is no altering, adjusting, or interfering with the breath because it is a natural function of the body. Allow the breath to be and follow its movement.

Mindfulness breathing returns us to stillness and our true selves. Practising this mindfulness breathing for 5-10 minutes a day is enough to provide a small taste of the peace and balance available to us.

The next step is to take this mindfulness breathing into our daily lives. Whether it is when cooking the evening meal, travelling to work, or picking up kids from late afternoon sport. It is being aware of the natural flow of our breath during these activities. In this way, we become present to ourselves, to others, and to the 'now'.

> REFLECT – What is the best time of the day for you to have soul time?
>
> ACTION – Sit comfortably in a straight-back chair, feet flat on the ground, hands resting gently on the lap. Close your eyes and for 5-10 minutes; become aware of your breath and be still. If this works for you, return to it for the next seven days and notice what occurs within you. Journal your progress each day. Read *The Miracle of Mindfulness*, by Thich Nhat Hanh. Also *The Power of Now*, by Eckhart Tolle.

JOURNAL REFLECTIONS

6. A Simple Way

Be quiet in your mind, quiet in your senses, and also quiet in your body.
Then, when all these are quiet, don't do anything.
In that state, truth will reveal itself to you.

KABIR

REFLECT – Breathwork is the easiest first step in connecting to our spirituality because it requires no rules, no teacher, no book, no class, and no equipment – just our body. Breathwork is a simple way of discovering the still point within us. There are countless options to choose from, and we select the one that is right for us. As in all areas of spirituality, there is no right or wrong way, it is about being true to ourselves.

ACTION – Suggested Breathwork:
- Consciously slowing down the breathing cycle.
- Consciously taking slow deep breaths through the nose and exhaling fully, and loudly through the mouth.
- Using four second cycle-breathing, in through the nose for four seconds, and breathing out through the mouth for four seconds.
- Breathing in and out through the nose.
- Being aware of our breath without changing it.
- Mindfully following the breath from the nose or mouth down to the diaphragm and back up again.

REFLECT – Formal practices may assist in mindfulness breathing, yoga, and Qi Gong

ACTION – Sometimes consciously connecting to your breath may be challenging or even anxiety-provoking. If this is the case, you can place your hands on your chest or stomach to feel the effects of the breath on parts of the physical body.

JOURNAL REFLECTIONS

7. Electric Train

You have power over your mind – not outside events.
Realise this and you will find great strength.
MARCUS AURELIUS

The ability to be still is central in approaching our soul. It can be achieved through breath work, muscle relaxation, guided visualisation, chanting, yoga exercises or just sitting. The challenge is dealing with our interfering thoughts.

Here are three simple strategies. Firstly, we imagine our thoughts as electric trains. We do not fight the thought train or attempt to control it, simply let it pass. We may see a myriad of trains flashing past us, and might even come across several that attempt to stop at our station. Just wave them on. Gradually, the number of trains begins to lessen until we enter our point of stillness.

The second approach is being aware of a thought and imagining it entering our head from the right side, near the temple, and focusing on its path across the forehead. Inexplicably as it moves the thought quickly dissipates and peace is found.

The third approach is imagining each thought as a balloon attached to a piece of string which we are holding. As we become aware of each thought, let the string go and watch the balloon fly effortlessly up into the sky, until there are no more balloons.

> REFLECT – The train thought, entry point, and balloon exercises are three examples of moving gently to a place of quiet. These strategies focus on developing stillness so the soul whispers can emerge.
>
> ACTION – Practise stillness every day. Attempt all three of these approaches with your thoughts, and see if one is a good fit.

JOURNAL REFLECTIONS

8. Our Three Closest Friends

Trying to understand is like straining through muddy waters.
Have the patience to wait! Be still and allow the mud to settle.
TAO TE CHING

Being quiet and listening to the soul murmurings requires three very special friends: patience, courage, and gentleness.

Patience is essential when we are learning how to be still. It is much like any new practice whether learning to play a musical instrument, speak a new language, or develop a new exercise routine; slow and steady wins the race. Each daily practice lays a foundation for our cerebral wiring and muscle memory and commences the gentle relationship with our soul.

Courage is required every time we are tempted not to engage in a period of quiet. Whether a novice, a seasoned, or a veteran practitioner in the art of being still, we all need courage to embark on the inner journey. This temptation to stop is born out of a fear of the internal mystery, of what may lie deep within. It takes courage to meet ourselves with compassion.

Gentleness with us is imperative. The pilgrimage inwards can and sometimes bring with it new insights, wisdom, and even strong feelings may surface. Gentleness will assist us to remain open to these revelations.

> REFLECT – Is today the day to commence this journey? Is today the day to return to your practice of having soul time?
>
> ACTION – Visualise where kindness, strength, and compassion are held in your body, and imagine them spreading through your being, from head to toe.

JOURNAL REFLECTIONS

9. On the Terrace

The creation of a thousand forests is in one acorn.
RALPH WALDO EMERSON

One of the wonderful advantages of living on the seventh floor of an apartment block is the gorgeous views I have of the wandering Brisbane River and the Western sky. As I sit on our terrace, I witness the crimson sunsets, the ebb and flow of the tidal river, the waxing and waning of the moon, and the flowering jacarandas.

At the end of the working day, I take five to ten minutes on the terrace to take in these sights, perfumes, and sounds. It is a way for me to slow down, to make the transition from work to home, and most importantly, to ground myself again on this beautiful planet.

A way of connecting to the intangible inner self is through our physical world. By connecting to the power, beauty, and silence of Mother Earth, we are gently nudged inwards to consider our place in the wider cosmos.

> REFLECT – What and where is your terrace? How often can you place yourself there and spend time? What in the physical world stirs your spiritual self? Is it a tree, flower, sunset, moonrise, water, rainforest, or mountains?
>
> ACTION – Every day, allow yourself a small amount of time in the environment of your choice. Allow yourself to sit or stand in this place and be. Journal how you experience each time you allow yourself to be still. This is all soul work.

JOURNAL REFLECTIONS

10. Lamb and a Clare Valley Red

There is no love sincerer than the love of food.
GEORGE BERNARD SHAW

Imagine sitting down to a plate of medium rare lamb cutlets sitting on a bed of mashed jack potatoes with a side of seasonal greens. The lamb is kissed with a garlic and rosemary sauce and the vegetables shine with a generous coating of olive oil and black pepper. Accompanying this dish is a glass of cabernet sauvignon from the Clare Valley in South Australia.

This is a feast for the senses.

The eyes are drawn to the verdant green of the vegetables, the pinkness of the lamb, the nose delights in the tannins of the wine, and the fat of the lamb. The taste buds are tantalised by the wonderous combination of garlic, rosemary, and olive oil as they infuse the ingredients on the plate.

What a wonderful occasion to treat this event as a mindfulness activity, engaging with each of the senses to live and cherish the moment. Pair this with authentic conversation with significant others, and we have a soul moment.

REFLECT – Soul or mindful moments are not necessarily a solo adventure.

ACTION – At your next meal, allow yourself to engage all your senses to truly live in the moment. Stephanie Bennet Vogt in her book *A Year for You* has a section on using the physical senses to connect with the inner self.

JOURNAL REFLECTIONS

SPIRITUALITY IN THE ARTS AND TRAVEL

11. A Place of Restful Contemplation

> There is nothing that art cannot express.
>
> OSCAR WILDE

All around the world, art galleries beckon us to embark on a journey to our soul, where we can explore meaning, hope, and mystery. These galleries are critical to the general wellbeing of individuals and communities because they mirror our experiences and attempts to understand.

The Gallery of Modern Art (GOMA) is situated on the southern bank of the winding Brisbane River in the cultural precinct across the water from the CBD. Its architectural design utilises the proximity of the river through its floor-to-ceiling glass walls which offer stunning views of the river and ample filtered light, to create an ethereal atmosphere.

Each visit to GOMA is a soul moment for me. The combination of spaciousness within the gallery itself, the quietness of the exhibiting rooms, the art, and the serene views to the river draw me into a place of restful contemplation.

This is the beauty and importance of art and galleries in our collective worlds; they whisper to our soul.

REFLECT – Where is your place of restful contemplation?

ACTION – Draw, paint, copy, or colour in an image that brings you joy. Take the time to let your imagination roam free. Connect to mindfulness in this pursuit. Visit your city's art gallery. Admire and critique the works presented, but also allow the space and time for the internal journey. Allow the experience to touch all parts of your being.

JOURNAL REFLECTIONS

12. A Doorway to the Soul

Music gives a soul to the universe, wings to the mind,
flight to the imagination and life to everything.

PLATO

Listening to Andrea Bocelli's, *Con Te Partiro* after my mother's death somehow gave expression to my experience of great loss and gratitude. The emotive tones and lyrics were a tonic to my grief.

In preparation for any workshops or ceremonies I facilitate, I call on the music expertise of Jimmy Barnes, Tina Turner, and ACDC. The songs – *No Second Prize, Simply the Best* and *Thunderstruck,* imbue my whole being with a wonderful sense of physical and emotional strength. Presenting becomes easier and more enjoyable with this grounding.

Former Australian prime minister Paul Keating commented he would listen to classical music to infuse him with confidence when presenting major policy statements, or when performing in the lower house of Parliament. Music was his inspiration.

Like the visual arts, music is a doorway to not only our feelings and physical selves but to our very soul.

REFLECT – What music inspires you? What music do you need when you are sad, happy, down, or anxious? What music takes you to life?

ACTION – Relax in your favourite chair and play inspiring music. Journal what the experience is like for you. This is your soul time. Make a playlist for each of your different emotional needs. Engage with a music therapist to discover the playlists that best support your emotional, physical, and psychological wellbeing.

JOURNAL REFLECTIONS

13. It's Not Your Fault

He pushes people away before they get a chance to leave him.
SEAN MCGUIRE IN *GOOD WILL HUNTING*

In the movie *Good Will Hunting*, Sean McGuire (Robin Williams) is counselling a wayward but brilliant mathematician Will Hunting (Mat Damon). Will is a complex and angry individual haunted by an abusive childhood.

Talking about his historical abuse, Sean says to Will, "It's not your fault". Will's immediate response is to shrug off the statement. Tension builds as Sean amplifies this through repetition.

Will, hearing the truth behind the statement, becomes annoyed, then angry, and physically shoves Sean away. Despite this aggression Sean continues to repeat, "It's not your fault". Will is visibly shaken. Sean again repeats the message. In a cathartic moment, Will breaks down and allows himself to be held in Sean's arms as the years of unshed tears and unfounded guilt are released.

From this authentic intervention, Will turns his life around.

Good Will Hunting is inspirational art as it taps into human experience, pain, and the healing power of authentic relationships.

This film reminds us of how cinematography can play a significant role in exploring our deepest experiences and yearnings. Films have the power to touch our souls.

REFLECT – What movies stir your soul and empower you to be your best self?

ACTION – Watch a movie that inspires you, and moves you to reflect on its meaning. Where does it take you? Other movies with similar themes or powerful messages are *Shadowlands, Dead Poet's Society, Billy Elliot, Field of Dreams,* Truman, *Hidden Figures, Mulan, The Quiet Girl, Calvary, Spotlight, Shawshank Redemption,* and *Wonder Woman.*

JOURNAL REFLECTIONS

14. Discovering My Home

The one thing in the world of value, is the active soul.
RALPH WALDO EMERSON

In 2002 as a young family we spent six months living in Limerick, Ireland. Though coming from a strong Celtic bloodline, I was still surprised at the deep connection I made to the people, culture, and landscape of the Emerald Isle. The humour, hospitality, and spirituality of the country tapped into my sense of history and identity.

While my wife taught at the University of Limerick, I cared for our two-year-old daughter, and together we had the time and space to breathe in the spirit of Ireland. During this exploration, a family friend gifted me the book *Anam Cara, Spiritual Wisdom from the Celtic World*, by John O'Donohue.

O'Donohue's work made a deep impression on me. His prose spoke directly to my experience of lived spirituality. He writes about coming home to ourselves when we fully engage in the solitude of silence. This returning brings us into union with all living things.

Without coming home to ourselves, we will never be at home in the world. This returning is predicated on developing a lifestyle of listening to silence.

> REFLECT – What other books and authors feed your inner life? What work has taken you to a more life-giving space? What book or author do you need to return to? Which of the arts takes you on your inner journey? How often do you allow yourself to feed on these riches? What is your relationship with music, visual arts, movies, and literature?
>
> ACTION – Make time every day to connect with music, art, literature or film.

JOURNAL REFLECTIONS

15. Look at the View, Kiddies

All journeys have secret destinations of
which the traveller is unaware.
MARTIN BUBER

A Blue Holden Kingswood was our favourite family car in the 1960s and 70s. Our Easter and Christmas holidays were spent in the car as we explored country Victoria, New South Wales, and South Australia.

Invariably, after hours in the car, squabbling would begin in the back seat. Mum, as a distraction, would frequently allude to the beautiful vistas of lakes, rivers, oceans, mountains, or valleys on display and remark, "Kiddies, have a look at the view". We were too bored and restless to hear the wisdom of her words.

While her refrain was a diversion to assist Dad in driving safely, she was also informing us of the beauty of the world. Mum was educating us about the value of travel and being present in the moment.

Her words often come to me as I visit places of great beauty. Examples include Milford Sound, the Grand Canyon, Tahiti, Sydney Harbour, and Uluru. The majesty of these physical places is nourishment for the soul as they alert us to deeper realities. They whisper about the power of beauty, the mystery of creation and the possibilities of the infinite.

Travelling to places of grandeur and wonder is a deeply spiritual experience, but only if we, "Look at the view, kiddies".

REFLECT – What has emerged for you when you have visited places of great beauty? How did this experience connect with your soul?

ACTION – At your next soul time, bring into your awareness your last visit to a beautiful location. What arises within you as these images come into focus? What whispers do you hear? Journal your reflections.

JOURNAL REFLECTIONS

SPIRITUALITY IN DEATH, GRIEF AND CHALLENGES OF LIFE

16. Walking With Death

Death smiles at us all, all a man can do is smile back.
MARCUS AURELIUS

In the Buddhist tradition, it is encouraged to reflect daily on one's death.

In our Western culture, there is sometimes an avoidance of talking and relating to death. Working in pastoral care in an oncology ward, I was frequently dealing with patients and families experiencing the frailty of human life. When patients finally died, I was surprised at how little the word 'death' was mentioned. 'He passed away, she is gone, it's finished, they have gone home, you are too late,' or a simple shake of the head.

Is this avoidance out of habit and fear? Habit, because as a society we lack the language and safety to talk openly about such things. Fear, because of the pain of grief and the mystery of what lies, or does not lie beyond.

Such an aversion, while understandable, is a shame as it prevents an authentic dialogue with the realities of life. In talking about death, we normalise the experience, we assist the grieving process, and we prioritise what is important in our lives.

Allowing ourselves to befriend our death, is another gateway to the inner life. Walking with death is not morbid or defeatist. In embracing this reality, we remain open to the mysteries of life.

REFLECT – May you find a place of warmth and welcome when your dear friend death, takes you by the hand.

ACTION – Read John O'Donohue's *Anam Cara*, Ch. 6, *Death: The Horizon is in the Well.*

JOURNAL REFLECTIONS

17. If I Had One Day

*I cannot escape death, but at least I can
escape the fear of death.*
EPICTETUS

REFLECT – How do you wish to live the remainder of your life? What is your purpose and direction? What is your relationship with death? Have you ever asked yourself these questions? The following activities will assist in reflecting on these themes.

ACTION – Reflection one, journalling exercise.
If you had one year to live, what would you do? If you had six months to live, what would you do? If you had one month to live, what would you do? And if you had one day to live, what would you do with this precious day? Pause after this activity.

Look at the list from the twelve months to the one day. Does the list become smaller as you progress? If so, why? Does this give you clarity about what is central in your life? If so, live your life with this focus.

ACTION – Reflection two, journalling exercise.
After a period of silence and stillness, reflect on a loved one who has died. Go over the last few years of their lives. Remember the key moments during this period and the way they interacted with you. Take this reflection to the point of their death, and then to the funeral or ritual. Focus more on the quality of your relationship with them and the goodness they brought into the world. In doing this five-minute reflection, notice what emerges. Does it offer further clarity about your purpose and direction in life?

This reflection is best when the grief is not recent or heightened.

JOURNAL REFLECTIONS

18. Good Grief

Grief itself is a medicine.
WILLIAM COWPER

Grief is deeply individual, and a completely cellular experience. Deeply individual, because we all do it differently. Cellular, every cell of our being is impacted. Each hug, kiss, and emotional connection is remembered in every atom of our being; conscious and unconscious.

Grief invites us, as we mourn our loved one, to review the meaning and purpose of our lives. Life is not the same, life has altered and challenges us to reconsider the world we have constructed. Grief innately draws us into the inner world, the place of the soul.

Grief asks simple questions. Where is my meaning? How shall I live now? What is important to me? What takes me to joy and life?

All existential questions take on a new sharpness when grief takes hold.

> REFLECT – There is nothing quite like the opportunity presented by grief. Grief allows you to go within and explore places of hurt, belonging, deep yearning, and unmet need. Grief presents you with an opportunity to grow and mellow.
>
> ACTION – Take your sadness to your soul time and listen. Grief counselling is a great opportunity to attend therapy and can be a wonderful support. Read *It's Okay That You're Not Okay* by Megan Devine.

JOURNAL REFLECTIONS

19. Upside Down and Inside Out

Pursue some path, however narrow and crooked,
in which you can walk with love and reverence.
HENRY DAVID THOREAU

For centuries philosophers, psychologists, authors, and theologians have pondered life's meaning and purpose. In his novel, *The Plague*, the existential author Albert Camus writes 'But what does it mean, the plague? It's life, that's all'.

Life can toss up many challenges: plagues, wars, divorces, Covid-19, accidental deaths, loss of jobs, unwanted pregnancies, health issues, miscarriages, economic recessions, and depressions. All of which have happened, do happen, and will continue to happen.

These events can challenge our internal world, where our previous understandings of life are turned upside down and inside out. Our life map is no longer current and we become lost.

We are challenged to create a new and relevant life map. To do this we need to sit with our experience of being lost and let the path emerge.

REFLECT – Allow the soul to guide you when faced with the challenges of life. Silence and solitude will enable you to listen to the murmurings of your spiritual self. Remember, slow down and breathe.

ACTION – Watch the movies *Life of Brian* and *Inside Out*. Read Albert Camus *The Plague*.

JOURNAL REFLECTIONS

SPIRITUALITY AND RELIGION

20. The Distinction

Any fool can know. The point is to understand.
ALBERT EINSTEIN

Religion is a set of beliefs, doctrines, and moral principles based on a specific God, Gods or teachings of a founder. Examples include the world religions of Christianity, Judaism, Hinduism, Buddhism, and Islam.

Conversely, spirituality is not about doctrine, belief, and moral principles but the experience of listening and acting on the murmurings rumbling deep within us. Religion focuses on adherence to a set of rules and regulations. Spirituality focuses on being true to the whispers we hear.

We are all spiritual but not all of us have a religion. Religion is only one way of giving expression to our spirituality. Unfortunately, this distinction is not readily understood and we can sometimes conclude because we do not have a religion or don't belong to a faith community, we are not spiritual.

To be human is to be spiritual.

Understanding this distinction enables a broader conversation about spirituality.

REFLECT – What is your understanding of religion and spirituality? Do you regard yourself as spiritual?

ACTION – Journal your definition of spirituality. Read *Beyond Belief* by Hugh Mackay.

JOURNAL REFLECTIONS

21. Talking Symbols

Symbols are powerful because they are
the visible signs of invisible realities.

AUGUSTINE

Over the centuries, religions have provided rituals honouring rites of passage: birth, belonging, coming of age, commitment, anniversaries, and death.

My favourite childhood ritual was the Easter Holy Saturday night which celebrated the life of Jesus. The ritual incorporated the lighting of a fire outside the church, symbolising the Light of Christ. As a young child, I was intrigued by the dancing flames and the sharp smell of burning eucalyptus leaves. With a candle lit from the fire, the community walked into the darkened church to symbolise Jesus bringing light into the world.

The soul is often confused by words, ideas, and concepts but we understand the world of symbols. As a child, I did not understand the theology of the Easter story, but I clearly understood light illuminates the darkness.

Water, wine, bread, and soil are other potent examples of spiritual symbols. Water speaks to us of life and cleansing. Wine of celebration and joy. Bread of sustenance and simplicity. Soil of growth and harvest. Used well, symbols speak directly to our everyday yearnings for belonging, nourishment, forgiveness and love.

Symbols are a gateway to our soul.

REFLECT – What religious or non-religious symbols take you to a deeper level of understanding? Which symbols speak to you of belonging, nourishment, forgiveness and love? Do your faith traditions use symbols that connect to your experience?

ACTION – Choose a symbol you relate to and focus on it for 5-10 minutes, notice what comes up for you in this meditation. Journal what emerges for you.

JOURNAL REFLECTIONS

22. The Silly Present

Where do we live symbolically? Nowhere except where we participate in the ritual of life.

CARL JUNG

Rituals were once the sole domain of religion. Not so today. As humans, we yearn to ritualise our lives and the key moments we experience. The common community action of placing a posy of flowers at a car crash site, outside a family home, or an office building when someone has died, is the often-unconscious desire to give symbolic expression to our deepest feelings.

The importance of ritualising is also reflected in many parts of our lives, often we call them family traditions: blowing out birthday candles, speeches at special events, annual family holiday, opening a bottle of champagne to celebrate an achievement, and even the Friday night drink after a week of work.

In the mid-1970s my parents started the family tradition of wrapping a 'silly present' for someone's birthday. The present is a simple cheap gift that is often funny, quirky, or silly in nature. The present has four clues and at the reading of each clue the birthday person guesses what the present might be. Laughter and frivolity result.

This 'silly present' tradition with all its silliness has a much deeper underpinning. The ritual and tradition is not so much about the words, the clues, or guesses but the interaction that takes place. The ritual brings people together to remind them of what is important: to love, to remember, to live, and to laugh. They return us to our core; our soul.

> REFLECT – What rituals do you have in your life? What do they say about you, and what is important to you?
>
> ACTION – At your next family gathering create a new ritual to share. Afterward, give yourself time and permission to pause and reflect on the benefits of the new ritual. Journal your experience.

JOURNAL REFLECTIONS

23. The Four Elements

Ritual expresses what lies deep within us.
ANONYMOUS

My professional career has centred at times on creating and facilitating rituals in church, school, and hospital settings from both religious and non-religious perspectives. These experiences have highlighted what I regard as the four key components of good ritual: symbols, participation, script, and community.

Inspiring rituals always use symbols and scripts that speak directly to our experience. They are relevant, accessible, and simple to understand, as demonstrated in the following example. At major Australian sporting events, a minute's silence is often used to commemorate and remember the life and achievements of someone recently deceased. This ritual is a most powerful example of a good ritual in action. It uses the simple symbol of silence: it invites people to participate by standing and being silent, a script that speaks directly to people's experience of loss and grief. Finally, it unites the community by the sharing of silence and standing as one.

Life-giving rituals invite us to connect simultaneously to both our inner world and the community in which we belong.

When we walk away from a good ritual we feel it. It inspires, gives expression to what cannot be put into words, builds connections, and energises us to live a better life.

> REFLECT – What has been the most inspiring ritual you have experienced, and what created this inspiration?
>
> ACTION – If you were to create a ritual for marriage, baptism, or memorial, what would it look like?

JOURNAL REFLECTIONS

24. The Good, the Bad and the Ugly

What is the essence of life? To serve others, and do good.

ARISTOTLE

Faith-based religions value add to our societies because they provide: ethical frameworks to explore moral dilemmas, philosophical foundations to probe life's meaning, rituals to nurture individuals and communities, and inspiration to encourage just and compassionate living.

Contemporary education, healthcare, and welfare systems in Australia are built on the extraordinary work of young religious women and men who came to our shores in the early 19th Century. This alone is a wonderful testament to the benefits faith-based religions offer our communities.

However, there is a bad and ugly underbelly to our faith-based religions. The litany of wrongdoing by our churches is profoundly disturbing. Misuse of power and money, mistreatment of the marginalised, the unequal treatment of women, sexual abuse, and moralising on ethical issues that exclude and alienate.

How do we marry such contradictory elements? We do not. We celebrate what is good and we name, condemn, and challenge the bad behaviour. Faith-based religions have their place in our society to assist individuals and communities to a deeper and life-giving spirituality. However, in some cases, they do the exact opposite. Their misuse of power creates a disconnect between what they preach and what they do. This does not promote authentic spirituality.

> REFLECT – What is your experience of faith-based religions? Have you experienced the good, the bad and the ugly?
>
> ACTION – What could you take from faith-based religions to apply to your life?

JOURNAL REFLECTIONS

25. The Pews Are Empty

I like the religion that teaches liberty, equality and fraternity.
B.R. AMBEDKAR

In Western society, our attachment to the church has been waning since the early 1970s. It is the first time in centuries we do not look for spiritual solace in the presence of a priest, minister, rabbi, or cleric.

There are reasons for this, however the most unlikely one, as expressed by some church leaders, is we have become less religious and more focused on material aspirations.

It is more likely, that we have become disillusioned with church leadership that is unable to listen. Sex scandals, outdated moral doctrines, and non-inclusive liturgies all repel those of us searching for truth and relevancy.

In response, we are searching in other places to find our spiritual nourishment. These include yoga classes, non-religious based mediation exercises, sporting groups, mind-body-spirit conferences, health retreats, tai chi, bushwalking clubs, or volunteer groups.

What all these activities and groups have in common is an ability to be relevant to our needs. This relevancy is about connecting to our deep desire for belonging, meaning, and wholeness.

When these basic soul yearnings are addressed, we experience a sense of community, purpose, and completion.

> REFLECT – What activities connect to your deepest yearnings? What brings you a sense of belonging, purpose, and completion?
>
> ACTION – Share these reflections with your family or friends and allow community to organically grow.

JOURNAL REFLECTIONS

PART TWO

ACTING ON OUR SOUL MURMURINGS

SPIRITUALITY OF HARMONY

26. The Contradiction

Who looks outside, dreams; who looks inside, awakes.

CARL JUNG

Part Two of this book explores how the nurturing of our interior life gradually propels us to live and relate in a different way. Our soul murmurings challenge us to authentic action.

As we care for our individual souls, we learn the lessons of the illuminators: grace, humility, and integrity. We learn to accept ourselves as we are, and we walk with greater gentleness and lightness.

This quiet revolution within ourselves then moves us forward. We feel motivated to live a better life not just for ourselves but for those around us.

The human soul cannot live when there's a contradiction between an enriched interior life and it not being mirrored in our relationships. When a disconnect occurs between the two, we are challenged. Do we listen and act on our soul murmurings, and alter our behaviour? Or do we choose to live in disharmony with ourselves?

REFLECT – What connection do you see between your inner life and the way you live in the world? Are you being challenged by your spiritual self to live differently?

ACTION – Take 5-10 minutes in quiet time to reflect on the above questions and journal your responses.

JOURNAL REFLECTIONS

SPIRITUALITY AND THE ILLUMINATORS: GRACE, HUMILITY AND INTEGRITY

27. Grace – A Noble Quest

> Be yourself, everyone else is already taken.
> OSCAR WILDE

As we attend to our soul life, we are challenged to live with grace. If we approach our inner self with shame and guilt, the murmurings remain silent. However, if we are open and loving to ourselves, we will discover the beauty within.

Being gracious with ourselves requires a certain gentleness. A gentleness free of judgement, expectation, and measurement. When this occurs, we relax into who we really are.

Being gracious with ourselves can lead to the discovery of an infinite bounty of gratitude. As we sit with ourselves and listen, we become aware of all that has been given to us. Life is a gift, even in our moments of hardship and disappointment.

To have grace with others is a noble quest. To have grace with ourselves is nobler still.

REFLECT – How do you approach your inner life? Is it with guilt, shame, and judgement or with graciousness? At this moment what are you grateful for? What are you doing when you are gentle with yourself?

ACTION – At your next soul time, sit with these questions and be open to what comes up for you. Purchase a gratitude diary and, on a daily or weekly basis, record what you are grateful for. On New Year's Eve read out loud all your diary entries. This can be done on an individual basis or as a family unit.

JOURNAL REFLECTIONS

28. The Challenge

For it is in giving that we receive.
FRANCIS OF ASSISI

Once graciousness finds a home within us, it starts to leak out into the wider world.

We sense ourselves challenged to show graciousness to all we meet no matter who they are: line manager, homeless person, waitstaff, our partner, and our colleagues. We greet them all with kindness and respect.

We sense ourselves challenged to be gentle to all, even the people who are vexatious to our spirit. We relate to them without judgement, expectation, or measurement.

We sense ourselves challenged to notice and appreciate more deeply the people who walk with us. We consciously honour them with our gratitude and love.

When we are kind, respectful, gentle and grateful we are living with grace.

REFLECT – As you journey along this path, your heart becomes bigger, more accepting, and loving. You are growing into your true self.

ACTION – Where have you been gracious, gentle, and grateful today? How did people respond to your way of being? Who has been gracious, gentle, and grateful with you today? Journal your reflections and share them with a significant other.

JOURNAL REFLECTIONS

29. Humility – Grounded in the Earth

Humility is the solid foundation of all virtues.
CONFUCIUS

My Year 8 Latin teacher was a strict man who had a passion for the ancient language. A passion I failed to share. However, I did learn the nuanced connection between the two languages from him. Understanding the Latin root of an English word brings its linguistic essence into clearer focus.

Two such words are humility and integrity.

Humility comes from the Latin word, 'humilitas', meaning humble, grounded, or from the earth.

As we journey into ourselves, self-awareness develops. We are not the centre of the universe. We are one of many, no greater and no less than any other individual. Being of this clay earth, we become aware we are finite, mortal and, like all others, a mixture of light, shadow, and contradiction. We are neither saint, nor sinner.

We seek to become grounded in this reality.

To boast, or enjoy the failures of others, to dominate conversations, or to be loud and aggressive, is not the way of 'humilitas'. Rather we learn to graciously accept compliments, we publicly rejoice in the other's success, we spend more time listening than talking, and we are gentle and courteous to all.

Humility beckons us into a new way of being. Grounded in the earth of our soul.

REFLECT – When and where do you feel most grounded? What is the quality of your presence in the world? Do you bring 'humilitas'?

ACTION – Go outside, take off your shoes and socks, and firmly ground yourself in the soil, the grass, or the sand. Spend five minutes connecting yourself to Mother Earth. Reflect and journal on this experience.

JOURNAL REFLECTIONS

30. Integrity – To Be Whole

> Knowing your own darkness is the best method
> for dealing with the darkness of other people.
> CARL JUNG

Like the word 'humility', integrity has an interesting Latin origin. It is derived from the Latin adjective 'integer', meaning whole or complete. To have integrity is to be undivided or unbroken.

How does this connect to our spiritual life?

When we journey inward, we can be confronted by our brokenness. Our soul offers a challenge: to love ourselves, even those parts which may be unpalatable. In accepting this and sitting with the shadow, we can experience wholeness.

This may seem counter-intuitive: to become whole as we embrace our fragmentation.

As we harness this 'integer', we not only accept our frailties, but we are called to lovingly embrace the brokenness of others. We simply become more compassionate and loving to those around us.

The embracing of this fragility has a secondary consequence – authenticity. We become more comfortable in our skin and at peace with who we are. The clearest expression of this integrity, and authenticity, is the connection between our motives, words, and actions, as they become one.

REFLECT – Integrity is best summarised by the character Polonius in William Shakespeare's Hamlet, 'To thine own self be true'.

ACTION – How comfortable are you in your skin? Is there a connection between your motives, words, and actions? How do you express your authenticity? How do you support others in their brokenness? Who do you share your fragmentation with? Take these questions to your soul time and journal your insights.

JOURNAL REFLECTIONS

31. Creating a Wave

In a gentle way, you can shake the world.
GANDHI

In the last four chapters, we have reflected on the illuminators of grace, humility, and integrity. These values have surfaced from the deep ocean within us. And like waves on an ocean, these qualities are sent from the deep onto the shore. What has emerged in ourselves, we now send out to others.

Each time we are gracious, humble, and authentic with ourselves, we send out a wave of positive energy.

And each time we are gracious, humble, and authentic with someone else we send out waves of healing energy.

Choosing to be still on a regular basis, creates a series of waves that wash over not only our world but the world of others.

> REFLECT – The creation of waves is all about motion. When you choose to live with these illuminators you create positive, pulsating energy to change the world.
>
> ACTION – In your stillness, be aware of yourself sitting by the ocean and watching the waves crash upon the shore. Breathe into these waves. As you do this, reflect on the waves created in you and sent out from you. How are you impacting the world? Journal these reflections.

JOURNAL REFLECTIONS

THE SPIRITUALITY OF SEXUALITY

32. A Tale of an Old Friar

Why does God give us this terrible, terrible urge?
ANONYMOUS

Three young friars and their 88-year-old mentor are casually walking around the cloister of their friary. As they chat, their conversation turns to the joys and challenges of living a celibate life. As the older friar listens, he nods knowingly with a pained expression on his face. One of the young novices noting his grimaced face, inquires as to the older man's thoughts on the subject.

Staring towards the ground, the elder religious man responds in a deep, gravelly, and broken voice, "Why does God give us this terrible, terrible urge?" The younger friars look crestfallen as they consider another sixty or more years of this terrible, terrible urge.

As bizarre as this story sounds I can attest to its veracity, the year was 1982. I was one of those young friars.

One can only imagine the celibate life of this older friar. His spirituality encouraged him to look upon his sexuality as a burden to endure. His natural desires and needs were not only unmet but deliberately suppressed.

An authentic spirituality encourages us to celebrate and cherish our sexual identity, desires and needs. How can we listen to the murmurings of our soul, if we have a spirituality that excludes our deepest yearnings for love and belonging? Our spirituality calls us forth to live life fully in all its dimensions.

> REFLECT – Spirituality will either promote or discourage a healthy sexual understanding.
>
> ACTION – At your next soul time, reflect on your experience as a sexual person. Bring your feelings, thoughts and yearnings to this place and allow yourself to be. What murmurings do you hear?

JOURNAL REFLECTIONS

33. We Are Beautiful

Become who you are.
FRIEDRICH NIETZSCHE

To enhance our sexuality, we need a spirituality that promotes the understanding that we are all sexual beings, with specific needs and desires.

Life-giving spirituality recognises we are beautiful as we are, and our sexuality is not defined by our physicality. Moreover, our gender, sexual preferences, and orientations are gifts which are to be celebrated.

Spiritualities and faith traditions that do not do this, cause harm.

Our sexuality and spirituality inform each other. Spirituality highlights the sacredness of our needs and desires. Sexuality challenges our spirituality to be authentic and empowering.

REFLECT – What relationship do you have with your body? How do your faith, religious views, or spirituality celebrate your sexuality?

ACTION – Affirmations which are best said with confidence, and out loud:
- I am a sexual being, with specific needs and desires.
- I am beautiful as I am.
- My sexuality is not defined by my physicality.
- My gender, sexual preferences, and orientations are gifts which I celebrate.
- My sexuality and spirituality inform each other.

JOURNAL REFLECTIONS

34. Illuminating Love

To love and to be loved is the only bridge to an authentic life.
ANONYMOUS

The values of grace, humility and integrity are precious gifts lovers can offer each other, they kindle both passion and authentic connection.

When we approach our lover with grace, it is without comparison or complaint. It is with gentleness and gratitude. We nurture our partner with kindness and celebrate their presence as a gift. Grace with our lover is always present when we choose to praise and honour them both privately and publicly.

When we approach our lover with humility, it is without arrogance or domination. We accept and love them as they are. We allow for light and shade. Humility with our lover is always present when we choose to see life from their perspective.

When we approach our lover with integrity, it is without mask or hidden agenda. We come as we are, authentic in our expression of thought, word, and deed. Integrity with our lover is always present when we name our feelings, wants and desires, and invite them to do the same.

Creating good authentic intimate relationships is not rocket science. It only requires a daily commitment of unconditional love!

> REFLECT – How are the illuminators present in your intimate relationship?
>
> ACTION – Sit together on a regular basis and have a conversation about your feelings, wants and desires. Journal your experience of this conversation. Read Susan Johnson, *Hold Me Tight*.

JOURNAL REFLECTIONS

35. An Intimate Partnership

Love cometh like sunshine after rain.
WILLIAM SHAKESPEARE

Being authentic with our sexual partner is a key in developing an integrated interior life. When we express our authentic self to our sexual partner and this is listened to and valued, we create life-giving bonds.

These connections are further deepened and developed in our sexual union. Sexual intercourse gives voice to the intimate bond that exists with our partner, and hard wires the loving connection to our brain and emotional system.

The euphoria we feel after an orgasm is a turbocharged connector. This connection is so much more than just a physical and emotional experience, it is deeply spiritual because it touches our soul.

And it is in this beautiful and deeply connected space where the internal lives of us and our partner can flourish.

> REFLECT – What is your sexual experience? What do you experience when you look into your partner's eyes when you orgasm?
>
> ACTION – After an orgasm, allow yourself to be, and experience the after effect. David Schnarch's book *Passionate Marriage* is a pivotal work exploring sexual, intimate relationships. Also read *A General Theory of Love* by Lewis, Amini and Lann.

JOURNAL REFLECTIONS

SPIRITUALITY AT WORK

36. The Lunchbox

Give evil nothing to oppose and it will disappear by itself.
TAO TE CHING

As we pack our lunch box for work, it might be worth considering placing the three illuminators next to the chicken wrap, crackers, and apple. As we put the lunch box in the staff refrigerator, we are reminded to work with grace, humility and integrity.

In doing so we enhance our chances of enjoying our work and positively impacting colleagues. Turning up to work each day with this intention creates an internal and external environment that is contagiously healthy.

This mindset, based on the illuminators, is the best toxicity antidote. Staff with noxious behaviour flourish in an environment where we collaborate in their negativity, divisiveness, and selfishness. If left unchallenged, this conduct becomes a cultural standard.

However, if we choose to not engage with these actions and instead reply with grace, humility, and authenticity, the toxic behaviour begins to wane. Like the foam sprayed on a fire it is smothered, and an environment of empowerment is created.

REFLECT – What are the values you take to work? What is your impact on the work environment? What is your current response to any toxic behaviour existing in your work team?

ACTION – At your next team or department meeting, observe the energy in the room, does it flow freely? Next time you experience toxic behaviour at work, try employing the illuminators and notice the response.

JOURNAL REFLECTIONS

37. My Opus

The only journey is the one within.
RAINER MARIA RILKE

Richard Dreyfuss plays an exceptionally talented musician in the 1995 Oscar-nominated movie Mr Holland's Opus. Mr Holland is composing his opus, a major original piece of music, however, he must accept a school teaching role to financially support his young family. Frustratingly these new commitments constantly interrupt his creative work. Over time, Holland comes to realise his great opus is not this composition, but his teaching and parenting roles.

If we follow the quiet whisperings of our soul, we can be surprised at how our career trajectory can spread to unknown and unexpected spaces. For all of us, some doors inexplicitly remain shut and other seemingly irrelevant doors will magically open. Like Mr Holland, this confusing professional journey may only make sense as we enter the latter stages of our careers.

If we follow the quiet murmurings of our inner life, we will recognise a recurring theme in all the roles, jobs, and courses we have done. Each has been a building block in creating our opus.

This masterpiece reflects the richness of our spiritual self and creates positive change in the world. Our opus makes a difference.

> REFLECT – What are the recurring themes in your education, jobs, and roles? What is the difference you are making? What difference would you like to make?
>
> ACTION – In your quiet time, reflect on these questions and your developing opus. Journal your insight and or thoughts. Watch the film *Mr Holland's Opus*. Read Thomas Moore's A Life at Work, which explores this theme.

JOURNAL REFLECTIONS

38. A Calling to Serve

Waste no time arguing about what a good man should be.

Be one.

MARCUS AURELIUS

Nelson Mandela chose to use his 27 years in prison to reflect on his life and prepare himself and his country for a new future. In a pivotal speech on his release from detainment, he expressed his gratitude to all those who championed his cause. There were no words of retribution or bitterness, just a commitment to be a humble servant of the people of South Africa.

Post-imprisonment, Mandela became President of South Africa and oversaw the peaceful dismantling of the apartheid system. Mandela confronted the structural injustices of his country with his goodness; a quality born and nurtured behind the walls of Robben Island prison.

Mandela offers a multi-layered template for contemporary leadership. Empowering leadership is born out of adversity, cultivated in personal reflection, and founded on grace, humility, and integrity. At the core of his leadership and the elimination of apartheid, was forgiveness.

REFLECT – Who are your leadership heroes? What are the qualities you admire? What kind of leader are you? Does your leadership have its foundation in your soul work?

ACTION – Become aware of how your leaders interact with the team. What do you observe? This observation is particularly educational during times of conflict and challenge.

JOURNAL REFLECTIONS

39. The Highest Priority

If your actions inspire others to dream more, learn more, do more, and become more. You are a leader.

JOHN QUINCY ADAMS

Great leaders do not seek positions of power, the position seeks them. They recognise their role as a responsibility rather than a privilege.

Great leaders step into roles without ever becoming it.

Great leaders will always use their roles to empower others to be their best selves. Seeking the greater good is their highest priority.

Great leaders stand in solidarity with the vulnerable, the unseen, and the unheard. They have clear energy, are approachable, transparent, and authentic.

Great leaders recognise leadership is a gift. They understand the principle of impermanence and relinquish their roles with grace.

> REFLECT – Not every great leader carries the title of leader.
>
> ACTION – In your soul work this week, reflect on the following questions. Do you identify with any of these qualities? If so which ones? How do you influence your workplace? Journal your responses. Read *Leaders R Us* by Andy Robinson, or *Some Achieve Greatness* by John Bell. Are you able to initiate a conversation at work about empowering leadership?

JOURNAL REFLECTIONS

DISCOVERING SPIRITUALITY IN OUR PARENTING

40. The Green Cathedral

Children learn more from what you are than what you teach.
W.E.B. DUBOIS

My spirituality has not come about in a vacuum, the seeds were sown as I witnessed my parents' journey. I remember as a teenager walking one night into my parents' bedroom and my father Tony, kneeling beside the bed, head bowed, saying his prayers. This image remains with me, a humble and vulnerable man before his God.

My mother Mary journeyed with cancer for the last 18 years of her life. Her first diagnosis was a turning point. Meditation, yoga and reading on spirituality became weekly activities. These endeavours broaden her understanding of faith and place in the world.

In the last months of my father's life, we had an extended family holiday at Foster Tuncurry. On a sunny winter's day, we visited the Green Cathedral at Tiona which is an outside chapel looking over Wallis Lake; an idyllic spot providing a reflective space in nature. Hand-in-hand, my parents sat quietly on the old wooden benches, looking through palm trees to the waters of the lake. I was moved by their intimate and gentle touch.

Mary and Tony modelled a life-giving spirituality. It encouraged me to be humble, accepting of my vulnerabilities, open to different views of the world, and authentic with others.

> REFLECT – The foundations of your spirituality are grounded in your family of origin. What did you learn about spirituality from your parents? What was their relationship with mystery, wonder and suffering?
>
> ACTION – For your soul time this week, reflect on these questions and journal your responses. If possible and appropriate, have a conversation with your parents about their spirituality.

JOURNAL REFLECTIONS

41. Reimagining

There are two things children need from their parents:
roots and wings.
WOLFGANG GOETHE

At times in my mid-teens, I privately questioned the wisdom of my parent's parenting. They didn't seem to have a clear understanding of my teenage world.

My parenting quickly informed me I needed a wider lens to critique my parents. I look back now and realise I was indeed blessed. I was clothed, fed, housed, well-educated and given a safe space to grow. Mary and Tony had a deep respect and love for the individuality of each of their five children. They were loving and generous parents.

As we parent, we are given the opportunity to revisit our childhood and see with different eyes. Eyes which allow us to gaze more gently upon our parents and ourselves.

When I have comforted my children at times of physical and emotional pain, I have also been given a window to recognise my childhood vulnerabilities, and what I needed. This new knowledge assists me to be more compassionately present to my children.

Taking our parenting and childhood experiences to the sacred space of our soul can create a reimaging of our past and present.

REFLECT – What is your experience of your parents' parenting? How does it inform your parenting now? Are you able to gaze more gently upon your parents and yourself?

ACTION – Today, become aware of how you interact with your children.

JOURNAL REFLECTIONS

42. Letting Go

Let goodness go with the doing.
MARCUS AURELIUS

I remember leaving our first-born child with her maternal Nonna for the inaugural sleepover. Delight and apprehension rose within me. Joy for alone time with my bride, yet fear of the unknown. Would our daughter settle and be happy without us?

As the night progressed, my fear subsided but in that instant of driving away from our daughter, it became clear letting go was going to be my faithful parenting companion. Parenting is a continual process of letting go from the first drop-off at day care, through school, into adulthood and beyond.

When we have a light hold of our children, we allow them to discover their individuality, future, and life path. Empowering parenting provides space for our children to develop their friendships, ideas, and views about the world.

This non-clinging intent is a deeply spiritual experience, as it speaks to us of impermanence, attachment, and a future yet to be. When we cling as parents, we do not allow the natural energy to flow, and the soul murmurings become a muted sound.

> REFLECT – What is your experience of having a light or tight hold of your child? What assists you to let go?
>
> ACTION – This week, take your letting go experiences to your quiet time and be aware of what emerges. Have a conversation with your children about their experience of your parenting.

JOURNAL REFLECTIONS

43. The Expert

Throw out your conceited opinions, for it is impossible for a person to begin to learn what he thinks he already knows.

EPICTETUS

Nappies and toilet training were not my greatest love in the parenting role. However, I learnt one valuable lesson. Both of our children learnt to use the toilet when they were ready. For all our coaxing, talking, and prepping, the skill was only achieved when they themselves were ready. It was their timeline and their story, not mine. They have taught me this same lesson in humility repeatedly. I might be the expert of my life, but I am certainly not the expert in the lives of other people.

Our children instinctively know when they are ready for a new chapter to begin in their lives. Parenting is about listening to the quiet whispers of our children, so we can support them in trusting their own instincts. The more patient we are in listening to our murmurings, the more we can listen to our children.

> REFLECT – How has humility played a role in your parenting? What have you learnt from your children?
>
> ACTION – During the coming week, notice what assists you to listen more attentively to your children. Take your parenting experiences to your quiet time. Read Steve Biddulph's *Raising Boys*, and *Raising Girls*. Watch the movie *Parenthood*.

JOURNAL REFLECTIONS

44. Building Blocks

Children are educated by what the grown-up is and not by his talk.
CARL JUNG

The following activities assist in developing our children's ability to listen to the murmurings of their inner lives. These seven suggestions create a wonderful spiritual foundation.

Ritualising key family moments: graduations, birthdays and anniversaries. Attending formal ceremonies: marriages, funerals, baptisms, and ANZAC Day.

Attending movies, delving into deeper themes. The following films have been building blocks in my own children's lives: *Mulan, Kung Fu Panda, Star Wars, Harry Potter, Moana, Ice Age, Narnia, Toy Story,* and *Inside Out.*

Visiting art galleries, museums, and reading myth and legend stories exploring creation, hope, evil, suffering, redemption, and love.

Giving our children experiences of different faith traditions, and ways of living. Allowing them to safely explore and experiment with these new ideas.

Providing opportunities and space to have meaningful conversations when questions arise naturally from our children's lived experience.

Modelling; being open to mystery and expressing vulnerability.

Teaching our children how to meditate; how to be and how to be still.

All these actions will promote an inquisitive mind and an open heart.

> REFLECT – The building blocks of an authentic spirituality are not taught but lived.
>
> ACTION – Journal how you are currently supporting the development of your child's spirituality. This week, experiment with one or more of the activities with your child.

JOURNAL REFLECTIONS

THE SPIRITUALITY OF SOCIAL ACTION

45. Making a Difference

Act as if what you do makes a difference. It does.
WILLIAM JAMES

Catherine McAuley, Mary MacKillop, Martin Luther King Jr, Francis of Assisi, Caroline Chisholm, and Mahatma Gandhi were all ordinary individuals with a unique combination of strengths and weaknesses. What sets them apart is the depth of spirituality which propelled them to have extraordinary outreach to the poor and destitute.

Whether it was the impoverished Irish or Australian children, marginalised African Americans, 13th century lepers, young single vulnerable women, or a struggling nation searching for independence, these giants of justice brought hope, kindness, and a better world. They challenged the status quo and demanded the unseen to be seen.

In listening to their murmurings, these legends of social action were driven to make a difference. Each created a wave of justice that continues to wash over our cultural shores.

> REFLECT – In your moments of stillness, do you hear whispers calling you to action? Do you act on these murmurings?
>
> ACTION – In your soul work this week, listen for the murmurings calling you to action. Read a biography of one of the people named above, or one of your heroes that has brought significant and lasting change to those who are less fortunate.

JOURNAL REFLECTIONS

46. In Exile

> I think my way of prayer is to stand in wonder at the beauty
> of people and the wonder of life.
> PETER KENNEDY

In the mid-1980s, Peter Kennedy became parish priest of St Mary's Catholic Church, South Brisbane. Under the guiding hands of Peter and Terry Fitzpatrick, over the following twenty years the community developed a spirituality and theology encompassing the gospel values of inclusivity and social justice.

Inclusivity was expressed in the welcome given to all people: the homeless, the divorced, members of the LGBTQIA+, and all others who were looking for a non-judgemental spiritual home. Women in the parish were given significant roles including preaching and leadership.

With the inspiration of community member Karyn Walsh, social justice was primarily expressed in the Micah Projects' foundation for the homeless. The parish also supported multiple community groups assisting the marginalised: those with disabilities, First Nations people, LGBTQIA+ people, domestic violence victims and those abused in church and state institutions.

The stance on inclusivity was a concern to the clerical arm of the Roman Catholic Church. Peter, Terry, and the community challenged the male leaders of the church to become more inclusive, democratic, and aligned to the teachings of Jesus. The official church, while initially ignoring some of these concerns, ultimately forced Peter, Terry, and the community out of the Parish.

The community still exists today under the name of St Mary's in Exile.

> REFLECT - Calling out injustices, challenging accepted norms, and inviting a more lateral view of the world can elicit anger, fear, and retribution. These can be the consequences of acting on your soul murmurings.
> ACTION - Read Peter Kennedy's, *The Man Who Threatened Rome*. Research Karyn Walsh and the origins and work of Micah Projects in Brisbane.

JOURNAL REFLECTIONS

47. Engagement

Arriving at one goal is the starting point to another.
JOHN DEWEY

I am always bemused when someone comments, "I'm not into politics". Politics permeates all we do.

We all wish to live in a society providing high quality services and assets for all its citizens, especially in the areas of transport, health and safety, education, employment, policing, and welfare. Who provides the funding, legislation, and processes for this to happen? Our political system of local, state, and federal governments.

To have the society and the services we desire requires engagement in the political process. Due to our inertia, we sometimes struggle to collaborate with the people and structures that provide for a healthier society.

Our need for quality services for ourselves, family, friends, and our fellow citizens comes from a very noble and sacred place: our inner world, our soul. When we listen to our murmurings, it challenges us to be involved. This is the fuel driving our sense of justice for a better tomorrow.

REFLECT – To choose to be engaged in the political process is an expression of integrity.

ACTION – Watch the following movies: *Mississippi Burning, Gandhi, Power of One, Invictus, Hidden Figures, Loving, Remember the Titans, Selma, An Inconvenient Truth, Suffragette, Iron Jaw Angels, Samson* and *Delilah,* and *Mabo.* Contact your local council, state or federal member and initiate a discussion on the social issues central to your life.

JOURNAL REFLECTIONS

BIG PICTURE SPIRITUALITY

48. The Light and Shade

Take only memoires, leave only footprints.
AUSTRALIAN ABORIGINAL SAYING

Boats, migrants, and heroes are recurring themes in our shared national story.

Over 75,000 years ago, our First Nations people migrated to the Australian mainland by canoe. Their relationship with the land remains a focal point of their spirituality. In 1788 the British arrived by boat with a different understanding of land and spirituality. In 2024 we continue in our attempts to honour these different voices.

Over the centuries, people have continued to arrive by boat, looking for a better life or an escape from oppression and poverty. We have developed a successful multicultural society, yet are still challenged by significant pockets of racism and bigotry.

We have a conflicted perception of our champions. Historically we have celebrated the defeated heroes: the ANZACs and Ned Kelly. We love the unassuming star epitomised by Karrie Webb, Ash Barty, and Sam Kerr. Yet we also celebrate the brash and aggressive hero who must win at all cost, as shown by some of our tennis, football, and cricket players.

These contradictory themes reflect the light and shade of our national soul.

REFLECT – What is your connection to the land? What is your experience of the Australian soul? What themes do you recognise? Who are your Australian champions?

ACTION – Ponder these movies as you reflect on the Australian Soul: *Rabbit Proof Fence, Gallipoli, The Chant of Billy Blacksmith, The Castle, Kenny, 10 Canoes, Mabo, Breaker Morant, Picnic at Hanging Rock, Muriel's Wedding, Strictly Ballroom, Ride Like a Girl, Sunday Too Far Away,* and *Australia*. Watch and reflect on the mini-series *Bay of Fires* and *Irreverent.*

JOURNAL REFLECTIONS

49. Holding Opposites

Respect for all and harm to none.
AUSTRALIAN ABORIGINAL SAYING

In Gestalt therapy, the counsellor invites a client to entertain the possibility of holding opposites. An example is attending to feelings of both intense grief and deep-seated gratitude during a significant loss.

Are we being challenged to hold the opposites of our nation's spirit?
- We are a welcoming and hospitable nation and challenged by the new and different.
- We are a democratic and equitable nation and challenged by a shared history of dispossession and poverty.
- We are a migrant nation and challenged by a notion some do not belong.
- We are a humble nation and challenged by the addiction to win at all costs.

As we listen to these opposing murmurings of our national soul, are we being challenged to become a people who:
- Celebrate diversity and difference?
- Are at one with the land and reconciled with the past?
- Believe in the fair go for all?
- Live and play with integrity?

> REFLECT – As an Australian are you called to be more than you have become?
>
> ACTION – Discuss with friends and family the topics of a national soul. Visit state and federal art galleries and museums to explore the notion of a national soul. What unique quality does the Australian nation bring to the global village? Read *Return to Uluru* by Mark McKenna.

JOURNAL REFLECTIONS

50. Surfing Lessons

Water is the first principle.
THALES OF MILETUS

I have always had a passion for the ocean and surf. They speak directly to my soul about how to live life.

Surfing is:
- A cleansing experience: physically, emotionally, and spiritually.
- Being one with the world and embracing its beauty and wonder.
- Listening to the whispers of the ocean and life.
- Rolling with the natural ebb and flow of all energies.
- Understanding the balance between adventure and safety.
- Learning collaboration and patience.

> REFLECT – Which of your passions speak to your soul? What have you learnt about your life and spiritualty through this passion?
>
> ACTION – At your next opportunity, plunge yourself into the surf and feel the cleansing waters rush through your entire being. Alternatively, mindfully immerse yourself in your chosen passion and be aware of what emerges. Journal your experience. Read *Mindfulness and Surfing* by Sam Bleakley and *Blue Water* by Wallace J. Nichols.

JOURNAL REFLECTIONS

51. Legacy

*There are two ways of spreading light:
to be the candle or the mirror that reflects it.*
EDITH WHARTON

We all crave to leave a legacy. A footprint to remind our loved ones and the world we existed and our life mattered. This legacy comes in all forms: buildings, companies, charities, children, trophies, books, music, artwork, academia, medals, trees, and gardens.

One of the most enduring legacies is the way we live our lives. The quality of our living reaches far beyond our contemporary generation. A life well lived is an echo resounding in all the world's tomorrows.

To attend to our spiritual self is integral to living a good life. If we choose to spend quality time each week listening to the murmurings of our souls, we will access an endless source of grace, humility, and integrity.

What a wonderful legacy to leave for future generations.

REFLECT – What legacy would you like to leave behind? Is it a legacy that will bring life to those who follow? Will it be a lantern in the darkness?

ACTION – After some quiet time, write your future obituary highlighting what you have achieved and what you have given to future generations. Watch the movie *Heart and Souls*.

JOURNAL REFLECTIONS

52. Touchstones

There is one spectacle grander than the sea, that is the sky;
there is one spectacle grander than the sky,
that is the interior of the soul.

VICTOR HUGO

Historically, a touchstone was a black quartz stone used to determine the purity of gold and silver. Use the following four touchstones to test the quality of any spirituality.

Solitude. An authentic spirituality is grounded in the silence of solitude. This spirituality creates a space for regular quiet reflection that is relevant and life-giving. This solitude can take many forms: mindfulness, meditation, prayers, mantras, walking on the beach, sitting quietly on the terrace, walking alone through an art gallery, rainforest, or bush track. It is in this solitude we learn to hear the soul murmurings.

Mystery. An authentic spirituality is walking with the mysteries of life and being able to sit with the unknown. This includes developing an open mind and heart, and an ability to hold our beliefs and opinions lightly. It accepts the light and shade of life.

Illumination. An authentic spirituality constantly radiates grace, humility, and integrity. This wellspring impels us to live a life of compassion and justice. True spirituality creates a better world.

Dynamism. An authentic spirituality is unique to each of us. It is never copied or borrowed. It comes from within and is always evolving. It is never static and never burdened by its past.

> REFLECT – What is your relationship with solitude and mystery? Are you currently living with grace, humility, and integrity? Is your spirituality evolving?
>
> ACTION – In your soul time this week, reflect on the above questions and allow your murmurings to surface. Examine other expressions of spirituality and test them against the touchstones.

JOURNAL REFLECTIONS

Conclusion

I want you to be everything that's you,
deep at the centre of your being.
CONFUCIUS

FINAL REFLECT – After reading and reflecting on these 52 chapters, what new insights do you have about your spirituality? Is there a chapter you wish to re-read? Is there an action you need to revisit? In what ways would you like to nourish your soul?

FINAL ACTION – During the coming weeks, go over all the journal reflections you have completed. Highlight the insights you would like to take into the future. Allow these to light your path.

ACKNOWLEDGMENTS

I acknowledge the writings of the following authors who have assisted in nurturing, shaping and developing my understanding of spirituality.

Michael A Singer, John O'Donohue, David Schnarch, Thich Nhat Hanh, Stephanie Bennet Vogt, J.R. Tolkien, Albert Camus, Tao Te Ching, William James, James Hillman, Carl Jung, Writings of Francis of Assisi, Catherine McAuley, Marcus Aurelius, Epictetus, Plato, Aristotle, Wolfgang Goethe, Thomas Merton, Hugh Mackay, Henri Nouwen, Joseph F Girzone, Wallace J. Nichols, Megan Devine, Arthur C Brooks, Thomas Keneally, William Shakespeare, Thomas Moore, Hector Garcia, Francesc Miralles, Sam Bleakley, Mark McKenna, Paul Callaghan with Uncle Paul Gordon, Oscar Wilde, Ralph Waldo Emerson, George Bernard Shaw, Friedrich Nietzsche, Henry David Thoreau, and Susan Johnson.

Thanks to the Queensland Writers Centre and in particular Vicki Bennett who has patiently and professionally guided me through the development of this manuscript. Vicki's sage advice, practical suggestions and encouragement has been highly significant. To my editor Ian Mathieson, for his incredible efficiency and eye for detail, my heartfelt thanks.

Thanks to those who read the manuscript at different stages and offered constructive feedback: Luke Kennelly, Robert Kennelly, Kate Vincent, Karen Atkins, Stephen Golding, and Forrest James.

To my professional supervisors and mentors Judith Floyd, John Barnaby, Forrest James and Peter Martin, who compassionately walked with me.
To my parents Mary and Tony Kennelly and my four siblings: Robert and John Kennelly, Barbara Crapper and Jenny Long, who not only provided my initial grounding in spirituality, but have continued to support all my endeavours. To the St Leo's, Mt Sion and Avila youth groups and the Franciscan Friars who expanded my understanding of what a contemporary spirituality might look like.

To my wife Jeanette Kennelly and our children Hannah and Isaac Kennelly, for their unfailing belief in me and this project. Their efforts, love and patience has been instrumental in the creation and completion of *Soul Murmurings*.

I stand on the shoulders of giants.
Thank you.

ANDREW KENNELLY – MY STORY

I grew up in the 1960s in the leafy eastern suburbs of Melbourne, in a typical conservative middle-class Catholic family. My world was Catholic; home, schools, rituals, and friends. The cultural revolutions of feminism, anti-conscription and the Beatles did not reach our front door until the 1970s. My lens to the world was constrained.

In Year 8, I was taught by a charismatic Franciscan Friar who presented a more personal, relevant, and engaging spirituality. From 1974 to 1979, I was a member of numerous school-based prayer groups that emphasised community, tolerance, and social action. My Catholic lens was beginning to broaden.

In 1980, I joined the Franciscan Friars, a Catholic religious order founded by Francis of Assisi. This 13th century man preached about feminism, ecology, and liberation of the poor; a man before his time. My 12 years in the Friars opened my eyes to a spirituality grounded in justice, humility and compassion. These are values to which I continue to aspire.

Two decisions I have never regretted in my life: joining and leaving the Franciscan Friars. Studying theology and philosophy, living in community as a celibate man, being exposed to a diverse range of pastoral settings gave greater depth to my developing spirituality.

In my last year with the Order, I fell in love.

While existentially painful, leaving the Friars was a life-transforming decision. My world has been enriched beyond measure through the love of my wife and the blessing of two wonderful children. Marriage and fatherhood have informed my spirituality about unconditional love, integrity and impermanence.

Professionally, I have aspired to take the Franciscan values of justice, humility, and compassion to each of the roles I have undertaken: educator, assistant principal, counsellor, healthcare professional and director of pastoral care. As a facilitator, I have led numerous retreats, workshops and rituals on self-care and spirituality. These professional roles and responsibilities taught me the importance of holding my beliefs and opinions lightly.

My personal and professional journey has predominantly focused on exploring the inner life. *Soul Murmurings – Living with Grace, Humility and Integrity* gives expression to this internal pilgrimage.

facebook.com/soulmurmuringsjournal